Grow Your Money Tree

A Beginner's Guide To Investing

GERAINT LIU

PARTRIDGE

Copyright © 2019 by Geraint Liu.

ISBN:	Hardcover	978-1-5437-5391-2
	Softcover	978-1-5437-5389-9
	eBook	978-1-5437-5390-5

All rights reserved. No part of this book may be used or reproduced by any means, graphic, electronic, or mechanical, including photocopying, recording, taping or by any information storage retrieval system without the written permission of the author except in the case of brief quotations embodied in critical articles and reviews.

This book is for your information only and does not constitute either financial advice or an offer, any financial decisions should only be made after consulting appropriate professional advisers, as everyone needs and investment objectives are different. Investment returns are not guaranteed. Investment involves risk and past performances does not reflect future returns. This book is not reviewed by MAS.

Because of the dynamic nature of the Internet, any web addresses or links contained in this book may have changed since publication and may no longer be valid. The views expressed in this work are solely those of the author and do not necessarily reflect the views of the publisher, and the publisher hereby disclaims any responsibility for them.

This presentation does not constitute either financial advice or an offer, any financial decisions should only be made after consulting appropriate professional advisers, as everyone needs and investment objectives are different. Investment involves risk and past performances does not reflect future returns.

Print information available on the last page.

To order additional copies of this book, contact
Toll Free 800 101 2657 (Singapore)
Toll Free 1 800 81 7340 (Malaysia)
orders.singapore@partridgepublishing.com

www.partridgepublishing.com/singapore

Contents

Introduction vii

How to Use This Guide ix

What Is Investing, and Why Is It important? xi

Step 1: Know Yourself 1

Step 2: Know the Five Types of Investments 7

Step 3: Learn the Nine Ways to Manage Risk 15

Step 4: Create an Asset Allocation Strategy 19

Step 5: Equip Yourself with Investing Strategies 27

Step 6: Understand the Power of Compounding 31

Step 7: Use the Power of Leveraging 35

About the Author 41

Introduction

Since I was a child, my mum has enjoyed growing money tree plants at home. Perhaps it's because a money tree plant is said to attract luck, wealth, and prosperity. However, just like any plant, it needs to be showered with the right amount of water and sunshine. Too much water can cause the stems to rot and the leaves to fall off. Too little water can cause the leaves to dry out.

But if you get it right, a money plant can live for more than fifty years with minimal care.

When I started my investment journey in my early twenties, I noticed similarities between growing a money plant and growing your money through investing: too much meddling or paying too little attention can result in huge potential losses. But if you do it just right, you'll see consistent gains, and the amount of wealth you have amassed through investing can last for generations.

In the next few chapters, you'll understand why, in today's world, it has become a necessity for you to grow a long-lasting money tree (i.e. a long-lasting pot of wealth) and how you can do so with the right amount of water and sunshine (action and inaction).

But first, let me share why I wrote this book.

Back when I was serving National Service, I had no idea what I wanted to do with my life. One thing I absolutely wanted was multiple streams of passive income. I wanted to achieve financial freedom.

I wanted to not have to worry about money, to be able to do whatever I wanted, whenever I wanted (such as live life on the beach, or travel the world). So I started my search for the skills and knowledge to attain this elusive, passive income.

I've spent countless hours on research and have sacrificed time with my loved ones to study the ins and outs of investments. I've spent tens of thousands of dollars on investing courses, both online and in person, and invested much more in different instruments, such as binary options, businesses, stocks, index funds, and mutual funds.

I made some of the most expensive mistakes yet made some of my biggest profits. Along the way, I met and was mentored by some of the nation's greatest investors, including Patrick Liew and Cayden Chang. Today, I'm grateful to have some of these successful people mentoring me on my investment journey.

But as I reflected on my journey, I realized many mistakes could have been avoided if I'd had someone guiding me from the start. Although, thanks to the internet, I had a wealth of information at my fingertips, I was overwhelmed with information and always wondered if I could trust the source.

I wished I had someone to tell me what worked and what didn't, what I needed to know, and what was just noise.

That is why I created this guide. The fact that you're reading it tells me you're committed but probably unsure how to get started—like I used to be.

I have compiled the lessons I have learnt from my personal experiences and those of my mentors, clients, and other successful investors I've met so you don't have to make the same costly mistakes I made and that you can more quickly accelerate your path toward financial freedom!

How to Use This Guide

Knowledge is NOT Power, it is only POTENTIAL Power, Action is Power.
　　　　　—Tony Robbins, Author and Life Coach

Many people learn without taking action, and they quickly forget the information. They may become more knowledgeable, but their lives do not change.

I want to help change that. I want this book to be more than a book; I want it to serve as a guide. Thus, I've created activities in some of the chapters. If you want to see any changes in your life, make sure you complete them.

To get the most out of this guide, I suggest you take the following steps:

1. Read one section at a time
2. Highlight and take notes as necessary
3. Take one piece of information from each section and immediately put it into action. If you can't, make a note to put it into practice as soon as possible.

Please do not just read this guide and forget about it. If you do this, you'll miss out on the guide's full potential!

Again, congratulations on investing in yourself. Just make sure you put your investment to good use!

What Is Investing?

As quoted by one of the richest men in the world, legendary investor Warren Buffett defines investing as "the process of laying out money now to receive more money in the future".

Basically, the goal is to put your money into a vessel in the hopes of growing it over time.

Why Is Investing Important?

As a financial advisor, I have met many people—some rich, some poor, and most fall in between. I've never met anyone who was rich who did not invest—all of them did. Whereas, regarding the poor and middle class, many have fears that hold them back from investing.

Let me share my experience with a client.

A man—let's call him Richard—reached out to me on social media, asking me to manage his finances. He was in his late thirties and earned about $4,000 a month working for the police force. He was single, still living with his parents, and he claimed that he spent close to nothing every day since meals were provided for.

Even though his expenses were few, he was saving only about $900 a month. Most of his salary went to his university loans, credit card loans, mortgage payments for his parents' house, and the money he gave his parents. He had no insurance or investments, just $20,000 in savings, yet his goal was to retire by 45, in seven years.

I asked him, "How are you planning to do that?"

He replied, "That's why I'm meeting you. I'm sick of my job, and I want to create passive income so I can retire."

But when I introduced the concept of investments to create the passive income he wanted, he shunned the idea. He was afraid of losing money. That's why he preferred to keep his money in the bank. But if saved his money in the bank since he started working, why did he have so little?

He then confessed that, besides his commitments, he spent money on vacations, dinner at fancy restaurants, and occasional new outfits.

What can his story teach us about the importance of investing?

1. A Better Future

Most of us are working jobs that we don't necessary like. The least we can do for ourselves is to make our money work hard for us while we are working so that we can reap the fruits of our labour in the future.

If Richard understood the importance of investing earlier, he would have been on his way to leaving his job and becoming financially free by now.

2. Disciplined Savings

Contrary to popular belief, the savings in your bank is not your real savings; it's deferred spending, meaning you'll have a high tendency to spend it in the future.

Investing isn't just a way to grow your money, it is a way to help you set aside money while you are busy with life so that you don't spend it on unnecessary things.

If Richard had set aside an amount to invest every month, he wouldn't been as tempted to spend on unnecessary things.

3. Get what you deserve

Many people believe that depositing their money into a bank account is the safest place they can put it and that it's never at risk. Many of us fail to realize that if your money is sitting in the bank, it is devaluing every year due to inflation.

For example, I remember when, ten years ago, a plate of chicken fried rice cost $2. How much does it cost today?

Do you realize banks lend and invest your money, taking most of the returns and giving you only a tiny cut?

You see, one of the key differences between the rich and the poor is that the rich learn to manage risk, while the poor either avoid risk or don't manage it at all.

In the next few chapters, I'll share how you can manage your risk like the rich do.

Leaves of Gold

Why Invest?

> Offers more choices in life
> Keeps you disciplined with your savings for your future goals
> Keeps ahead of inflation

Step 1

Know Yourself

Back in 2017, cryptocurrency (e.g. Bitcoin) was a huge trend.

I was approached by friends who offered me the opportunity to invest in coins of a different nature. One claimed that he had doubled his investment in six months!

I was in disbelief, so he showed me his account. It had grown from $20,000 to $40,000 in such a short time span! It was insane but apparently common in the world of cryptocurrency. He encouraged me to invest with him, but a gut feeling told me not to.

Eventually, in 2018, the cryptocurrency market crashed, and I never heard from him again.

No single investing strategy or approach fits everyone. I didn't invest in Bitcoin because it was beyond my parameters in terms of risk tolerance, time, and knowledge.

So how do you know if an investment vehicle suits you? You have to know yourself.

Here's a guideline you can use:

- **Goals**

It is fine to have different investments for different goals. The key is knowing the purpose of your investment and the results you're seeking.

Here's a list of questions to ask yourself:

1. What are your objectives?
___
___
___
___

2. Why do you want to achieve them?
___
___
___
___

3. When do you want to achieve them?
___
___
___
___

4. How important is achieving those goals?
___
___
___
___

- **Risk Tolerance**

Your investments should be aligned with the timeframe in which you'll need the money.

Here are some questions to guide you in determining your risk profile:

1. What are the average returns a year you reasonably expect to achieve from your investment portfolio?
    1) 2–3.5 per cent
    2) 3.5–5 per cent
    3) 5–6.5 per cent
    4) 6.5–8 per cent
    5) > 8 per cent

2. If the investment drops by 15–20 per cent over a year, you would most likely
    1) sell the whole investment
    2) sell part of the investment
    3) hold the investment
    4) buy cautiously
    5) buy aggressively

3. What is the acceptable level of losses you are able to accept?
    1) 8 percent
    2) 14 percent
    3) 20 percent
    4) 30 percent
    5) 40 percent

Add up the total number of points and refer to the risk profile chart below. For example, if you selected option three for all three questions, it means you have scored nine points and that you are Balanced.

Risk Profile Score

- 13–15 Aggressive
- 11–14 Moderately aggressive
- 7–10 Balanced
- 5–7 Moderately conservative
- 3–5 Conservative

Investing Frequency

How long would you want to stay in an investment vehicle (eg. stocks, funds, bonds, gold, foriegn exchange (forex), options, real estate)?

Some investors prefer to buy and sell on a daily basis, while some investors, like Warren Buffett, buy and hold stocks for the long term.

Both methods have pros and cons.

Buying and selling fast, also known as trading, allows you to take your profits quickly, but it usually requires a vehicle that has a lot of volatility (eg. Foreign Exchange(FOREX), Small Capitalisation Stocks)

The more volatile the market, the quicker one can make money. But that also means it's quicker to lose money.

The buy-and-hold strategy allows you to stay invested without being affected by short-term market fluctuations, but that also means you have to be prepared to leave your money in a vehicle for the long term. How long you decide to hold on depends on your goals, timeframe, and preferences.

Time and Knowledge

Some investment outlets require time to monitor and acquire sophisticated expertise and knowledge, while others are more of the set-and-forget kind.

What you plan to invest in should be based on how much time you are willing to devote to researching methods.

Some vehicles that require sophisticated knowledge are stocks, forex, options and real estate.

Some vehicles that are great for beginners include index funds, exchange traded funds, and mutual funds, all of which have professional fund managers who can help you invest in large parts of the market like domestic and foreign stocks and bonds.

Does that sound complex? Don't worry. We'll explain the different types of investments in the next chapter.

The point here is to only invest in things you understand and avoid things you don't. If you do your research, there is very little you won't understand.

Leaves of Gold

Be clear about your investing objectives.
Know how much risk you can tolerate.
Know the time period you are willing invest for.
Know how much time and effort you want to devote when it comes to investing.

Step 2

Know the Five Types of Investments

There are many types of investment vehicles out there. So how do you know which is for you?

As this guide is for beginners, I'll share some of the most common types of investments to start with.

Stocks

As a company grows, it issues shares to the public to raise money to operate and grow the business. A stock is a share in the ownership of a company. It indicates that the holder of a stock (aka a shareholder) has bought a piece of the company and has claims to its assets and earnings. Stocks are mostly bought and sold on stock exchanges like the Singapore Exchange (SGX).

There are two main types of stocks: common stock and preferred stock.

The 3 main differences between preferred and common stock is that firstly, a preferred stock gives no voting rights to shareholders while a common stock does.

Secondly, preferred shareholders have priority over a company's dividends before common shareholders.

Lastly, common shareholders will be paid out after creditors, bondholders, and preferred shareholders if the company goes bankrupt.

Bonds

Issuing bonds is another way companies and governments can raise money.

Bondholders are lenders of money to borrowers (usually a company or a government).

The borrower issues a bond, which includes the terms of the loan, such as the amount of interest payments and when the interest and principal (aka initial loan amount) will be paid.

The interest payment (aka coupon) is part of the returns that the bondholder earns for lending money to the borrower.

In the event the company goes bankrupt, bondholders will be given the highest priority to access the company's assets, followed by preferred stockholders and, finally, the common stockholders.

This implies that stocks are risker than bonds. And with lesser risk come lesser returns. Thus, bondholders are only entitled to receive returns from the interest rate, while shareholders can enjoy unlimited returns from dividends distributed from the company's profits and from capital gains by selling off their shares.

REIT

A real estate investment trust (REIT) is a company that owns, operates, or finances income-producing properties.

REITs are professionally managed within the company, which means you have to pay a fee for the management of your funds.

Pros

Predictable Cashflow

REITs are required to give out 90 per cent of their income as dividends. Investors should feel fairly certain they would consistently get dividends, as long as the REIT continues to make money.

Liquidity

Compared to traditional real estate, where it could take a long time to buy and sell, REITs are easy and fast to change hands as they are traded on stock exchanges.

Cons

Little Capital Appreciation

Because REITS are required to pay out 90 per cent of their income to their investors, they won't have much left to reinvest into their own portfolio. Hence, it can remain stagnant for years.

ETF

An exchange-traded fund (ETF) is a basket of vehicles (aka securities, such as stocks) that can be bought and sold on a stock exchange.

Its main purpose is to track the performance of an index, which is a smaller sample size of the overall market. For example, it's impossible to track every single company in Singapore. Thus, the FTSE Straits Times Index (STI) was developed. It tracks the top thirty companies in Singapore.

Since it is impossible to invest in an index, funds like ETFs are created to track the performance of the index. For example, some

ETFs that focus on tracking the STI are the SPDR STI ETF and the Nikko AM STI ETF.

Pros

Liquidity

Since it's traded on an exchange, you can easily buy and sell your holdings of an ETF.

Diversification

Compared to owning an individual stock, which can decline substantially at any time, an ETF encompasses a large number of stocks.

Some ETFs own stocks across multiple sectors and countries. So if one stock declines, the rest of the stocks act as a cushion.

Lower Fees

Compared to actively managed funds like mutual funds, an ETF is passively managed, meaning it incurs lower transaction costs and management fees.

Cons

Overdiversification

Due to an ETF's diversification, the returns are limited to the performance of an index and are dragged down by poorer-performing stocks in the index.

Investors could miss out on potentially higher returns, such as when you own a stock or a mutual fund that has a higher growth potential.

Mutual Funds

A mutual fund is an investment vehicle that pools money from investors and invests in securities like stocks and bonds.

There are two types of mutual funds:

- Actively managed funds
    o Professional fund managers pick investments according to the fund's objectives.
- Passively managed funds
    o An index fund is a good example of a passively managed fund. Its main purpose is to track an index, just like an ETF, but it is not traded on an exchange.

Pros

Liquidity

Mutual funds can easily be bought and sold.

Diversification

Just like an ETF, mutual funds own stocks across multiple sectors and countries. Some even own different asset classes, such as stocks and bonds combined. So if one security doesn't do well, investors will be unfazed.

Professional Management

A team of professional analysts and fund managers will help you pick out and monitor the investments so that investors can leverage their expertise and don't have to spend time monitoring their portfolios.

Convenience

If you were to invest on your own, you would have to spend time researching various securities. You would have to incur large fees to own as many securities as a mutual fund. You would have to monitor these securities as well. A mutual fund is great for people who don't have the time to micromanage their portfolios.

Reinvestment of Income

Most mutual funds allow you to reinvest your interests and dividends. This allows you to grow your portfolio without paying extra transaction fees.

Cons

Fees and Expenses

Because most mutual funds are actively managed by more people, you have to be prepared to pay for additional transaction costs and management fees, as compared to owning an ETF.

Over Diversification

Just like an ETF, the performance of a mutual fund can be dragged down by poorer-performing stocks in the fund.

Investors could miss out on potentially higher returns, if you own a stock that has a higher growth potential.

The difference between an ETF and a mutual fund's return is that a mutual fund's return is not limited to the performance of the index.

Leaves of Gold

Stocks
    A share of ownership in the company
    Higher risk and returns than bonds
Bonds
    Bondholders lend money to bond issuers
    Lesser risk and returns than stocks
REITS
    Owns and operates income-producing properties
ETF
    A basket of vehicles that can be bought and sold on a stock exchange.
Mutual Funds
    Professionally managed funds

Step 3

Learn the Nine Ways to Manage Risk

1. Education

Is driving a car risky if you haven't taken a test or practiced driving a car before? Of course it is! That's why it's compulsory to take your theory tests and practical tests before you get your licence.

Equipping yourself with knowledge before investing, like reading this book, is a great way to reduce your risk. Other ways to gather knowledge include investing in courses, speaking to investment professionals, and reading free online materials.

2. Stay up-to-Date

If you know what's going on in the market, and the global, industry, and company news, you can be better prepared to make decisions and position your money accordingly to take advantage of opportunities or prevent losses.

3. Insurance

Insurance is one of the best ways to reduce investment risk. If you are hospitalised and have insurance, you wouldn't need to sell off your investments to pay your medical bills.

Ensure you have at least the total permanent disability and critical illness coverage. That insurance is to replace your income in case you become permanently disabled or fall critically ill. You wouldn't want to be in a position where you are forced to sell your investments at a loss.

4. Invest for the Long Term

Did you know that if you invested in the S&P 500 Index, which is the top five hundred stocks in the United States, you would have gotten 9–10 per cent returns on your capital every year?

Having a long-term view prevents you from making decisions emotionally, and history has proven that the longer you invest, you higher your chance of making money in the long term.

5. Dollar Cost Averaging

This method, which is basically investing a fix amount of money at regular periods of time, is advocated by Warren Buffett.

The idea is that you'll buy more units when the market is down and fewer units when the market is up, lowering the average cost of one unit.

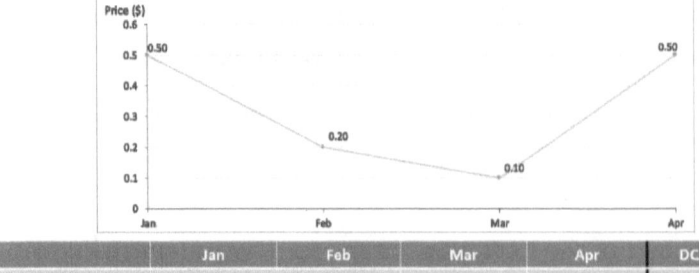

	Jan	Feb	Mar	Apr	DCA	Lump Sum
Invested	$1	$1	$1	$1	$4	$4
Price	$0.50	$0.20	$0.10	$0.50		
Units	2	5	10	2	19	8
Avg Price of 1 Unit					$0.21	$0.5

For example, if you invested one dollar every month for four months, you would have accumulated nineteen units, with an average price of twenty-one cents.

Whereas, if you invested four dollars on the very first month, you would have only accumulated eight units, and your average price of one unit would be fifty cents.

6. Follow the Trend

You can reduce the risk by only investing in stocks or funds that are in the uptrend. Just riding the wave can sometimes be the safest yet most lucrative move.

7. Stop Loss Orders

If you fear your funds dropping by a certain percentage, you can place stop loss orders so that the brokers will sell your holdings at the price you want. For example, if you can only handle a drop in your stocks of 50 per cent, you can set a stop loss order with the broker, who will sell it when it reaches the price you set.

8. Diversification

Create a portfolio of vehicles that are inversely related, so if the security falls, it does not affect the rest of the portfolio.

This diversification strategy can spread across not just different stocks but different sectors, countries, and asset classes too.

Did you know that bonds and gold are inversely related to stocks?

When stock prices are falling, investors are selling away their stocks and they tend to invest in safer assets like bonds and gold, as they feel that they have less volatility compared to stocks.

That is why bonds and gold price rise when the stock market crashes.

One of the best ways to diversify with small amounts of money is through funds, as we discussed earlier.

9. Asset Allocation

Create a portfolio of different asset classes.

How do you do that? What's the mix of asset classes your portfolio should be in? I'll share this information with you in the follow chapters.

Step 4

Create an Asset Allocation Strategy

Now that you know the different types of instruments and ways to manage risks, how do you put *all* of it together to form your own portfolio?

This is where having an asset allocation strategy comes in handy.

Here's the rule of thumb:

One hundred minus your age = per cent of the portfolio that should be in stocks

However, some experts predict that most of us will live longer. So if you have a larger risk appetite, you can change the number to 110 minus your age or 120 minus your age.

For example, if you are thirty, the percentage of your portfolio that should be in stocks would be 70 per cent (one hundred minus thirty).

If you are 50 years old, the percentage of your portfolio that should be in stocks would be 50 per cent (one hundred minus fifty)

This means your risk tolerance decreases with age as you have lesser chances to fail if the market crashes.

In summary, the following is how your portfolio should look as you grow older.

Ages 20 to 30

Pros

>Less commitment
>More time to recover any potential losses

Cons

>Low salary

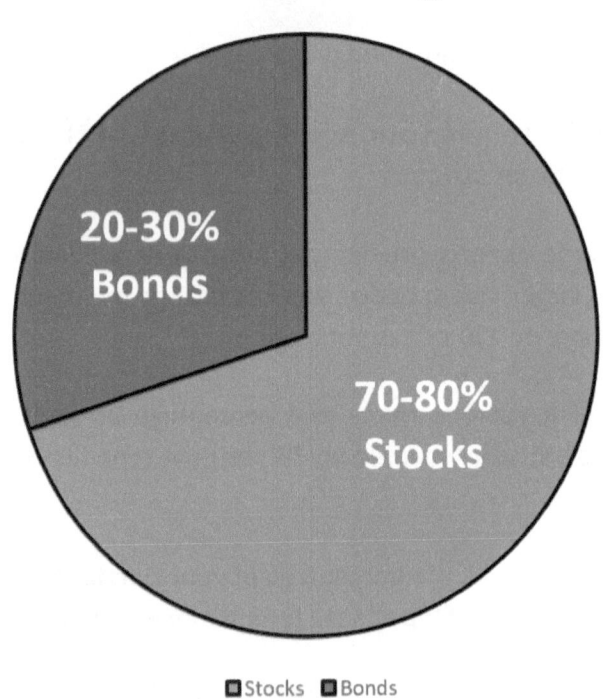

Ages 30 to 40

Pros

> Increased income
> Enough time to recover any potential losses

Cons

> Higher commitments: mortgage, children's expenses

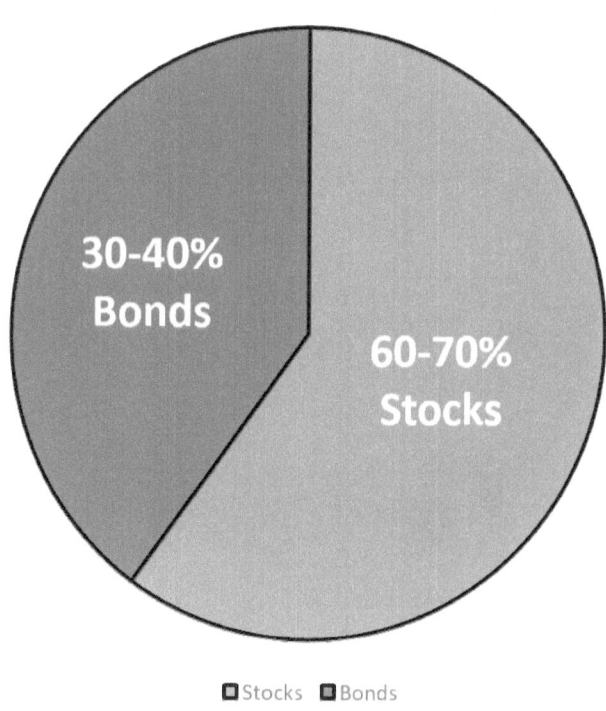

Ages 40 to 50

Pros

Peak of income

Cons

Higher commitments: child's university education
Less time for retirement planning
Less time to recover any potential losses

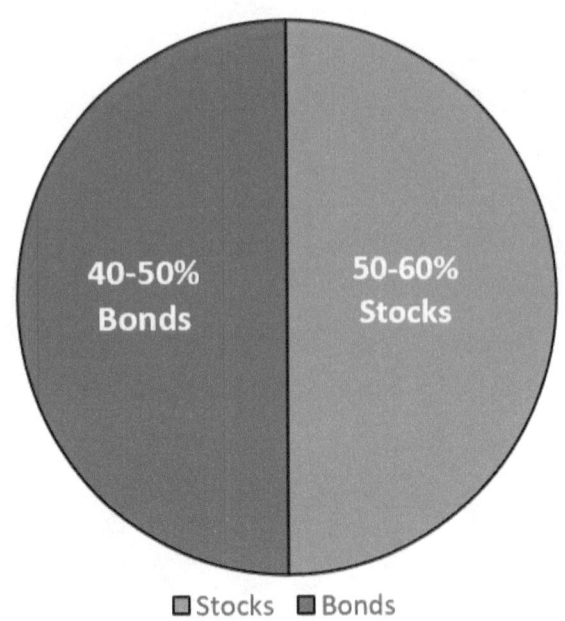

Ages 50 Onward

Pros

Accumulated good amount of savings

Cons

Increasing medical cost
Little time for retirement planning
Little time to recover potential losses

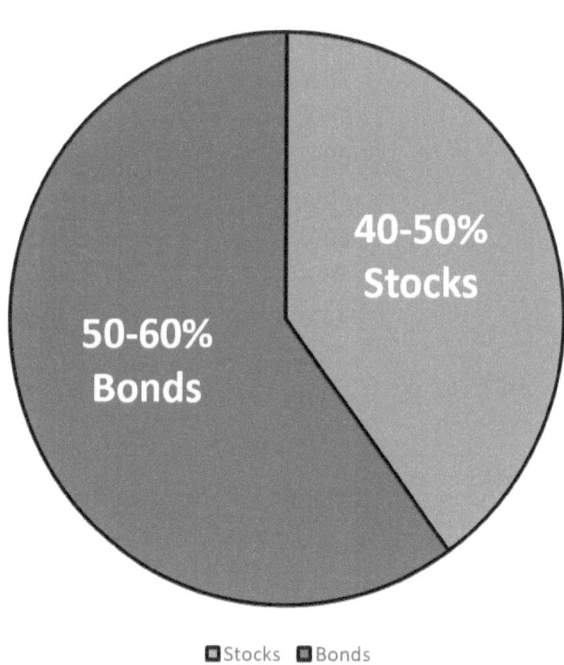

The Proper Asset Allocation Of Stocks & Bonds By Age
Conventional Model

Age	Stocks	Bonds
0 - 25	100%	0%
30	70%	30%
35	65%	35%
40	60%	40%
45	55%	45%
50	50%	50%
55	45%	55%
60	40%	60%
65	35%	65%
70	30%	70%
75+	25%	75%

Source: FinancialSamurai.com

Leaves of Gold

Construct your portfolio based on this formula:
One hundred minus your age = per cent of the portfolio that should be in stocks

Step 5

Equip Yourself with Investing Strategies

If you want to dive deeper into the type of stocks to own or the strategy to use based on your portfolio, this information will come in handy.

1. Growth investing

This strategy focuses on capital appreciation. The key principle of this strategy is to buy high and sell higher.

Growth investors look for companies that show signs of high rates of potential growth in their revenues and profits. A growth investing portfolio usually consists of stocks of smaller companies that have high opportunities for growth.

2. Value Investing

This strategy was popularized by Warren Buffett. The key principle is to buy stocks that are "cheaper than they should be".

By finding companies that are undervalued, investors have the potential to make big gains when the company becomes properly valued by the market.

Finding stocks requires skills and knowledge on fundamental analysis and calculating the true value of the stock, which can be quite subjective. A value investing portfolio usually consists of stocks that are deemed undervalued by the investor.

3. Income Investing

Income investing involves buying securities that pay you a steady stream of income.

An income investing portfolio is usually made up of a combination of bonds with fixed interests and securities that pay you high dividends, such as dividend stocks, mutual funds, REITs, and real estate.

How do you pick the strategy that fits you best?

Ask yourself what your goals, risk tolerance, and your timelines are.

If you are in your forties and are investing for your retirement, perhaps income investing may be more suited for you as it would give you a steady stream of income.

If you are in your twenties or thirties and don't mind taking slightly more risk for more gains, you might consider growth or value investing.

Leaves of Gold

Growth Investing
    Focuses on finding stocks with high capital appreciation
Value Investing
    Focuses on finding undervalued investments
Income Investing
    Focuses on finding investments that pays you a steady stream of income

Step 6

Understand the Power of Compounding

I once met a 55-year-old man. He had a wife, a 2-year-old child, and $10,000 in savings. He made about $5,000 a month and saved $3,000 of it. He told me he wanted to retire in ten years, with a passive income of $3,000 a month for the rest of his life.

I asked him how he planned to do that.

He told me he was going to build a portfolio of REITs from scratch. But he had no idea how to do it.

Unfortunately, if you do the math, with only $10,000 in savings, even if 100 per cent of his money was invested into the best REITs, it would be close to impossible to generate a passive income of $3,000 a month for the rest of his life.

He started investing too late.

In this chapter, we're going to explore how compound interest affects your investments in the long run.

Compound interest is basically interest on interest. Think of it this way: when you roll a snowball downhill, it gets bigger and bigger, right? And how big the snowball gets by the time it reaches the bottom of the hill is determined by the length of the hill. So the longer time the snowball has to roll, the bigger the snowball will be.

Same goes with your money. The longer the time your money is invested in the market, the more your money will grow.

Let's take a look at this example:

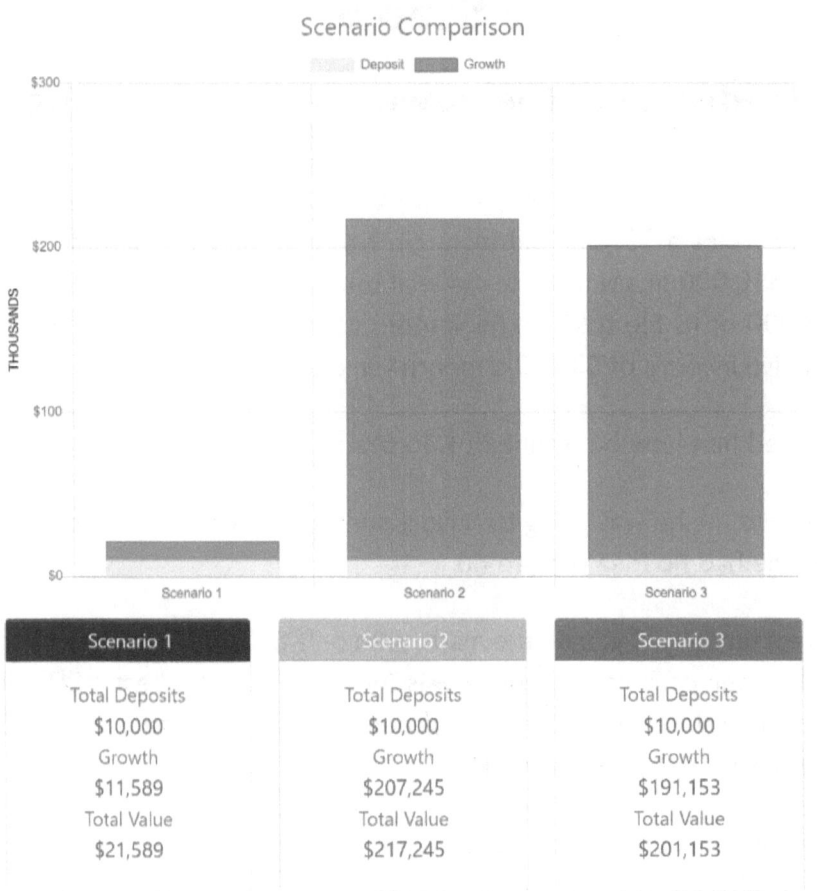

Refer to scenario one of the chart. If he invested $10,000 at age 55 in a REIT that gives him 8 per cent/year, he would get $21,589 at age 65.

In scenario two: if he invested $10,000 at age 25 in a REIT that gives him 8 per cent/year, he would get $217,245 at age 65!

Every year you delay is hundreds if not thousands of dollars lost in opportunity cost (the amount of money you could have earned if you'd invested your money).

In scenario three of the chart: if he invested $10,000 at age 26 (only one year later) in a REIT that gives him 8 per cent/year, he would get $201,153 at age 65!

That's a difference of **$16,092!**

Leaves of Gold

Invest early, and take advantage of the power of compounding.

Step 7

Use the Power of Leveraging

This chapter refers to a bonus tip, one that only successful people know, understand, and apply: the power of leverage.

Let me share a story.

Having lost thousands in investing in different vehicles, and trusting the wrong people, I eventually only trusted myself. I would spend hours researching and studying the different types of investment strategies and spend even more hours picking a particular stock before I invested in it.

Once I picked the particular stock, I monitored it every day. I read global, industry- and company-specific news, waiting for updates. At the end of the year, when the dividends came in, it was satisfying but somehow not rewarding enough..

I only made a few hundred dollars from my dividends after spending so much time researching and monitoring my portfolio. On top of that, I sacrificed time with my loved ones because I was so caught up with managing my investments.

My financial advisory business also took a hit because I was so focused on investing that I neglected my clients and failed to reach out to more people.

I thought, *If I live like this every single day, it won't be passive income anymore, it'll be active income.*

I still had to work for money. I had to spend time studying different investing strategies and vehicles as well as monitoring them for the rest of my life.

What if there's a way to automate this, or delegate this task, so I don't have to spend so much time researching and monitoring, and I can spend more time on my business and doing what I truly want?

That was when I stumbled on the power of *leverage*. You see, we all have twenty-four hours a day, and the rich understand that if you want to become richer, you need to free up time, because your time is worth money.

The only way to do that is to buy time through leveraging on people's time, expertise, and money—which is what I did. I delegated my investing process out to fund managers. I invested in ETFs, index funds, and mutual funds.

Although it is true, I could have gotten more returns myself, and they cost me much higher fees, but it was worth it. Because now I have time to grow my business, spend more time with my loved ones, and do the things I've always wanted to do, like travelling the world.

And that's what the rich and successful do—they buy time. They focus on saving time rather than saving money.

For example, one of my clients used to be focused on managing his investments, and he earned about $3,000 a month as an engineer. When he delegated the investment process, he freed up time for additional side hustles and developing. He eventually got better job opportunities. One year later, he earns about $6,000 a month.

That's an additional $36,000 a year!

That's the power of leverage.

Now, if you still want to manage your own investments, that's perfectly fine. I still own a couple of stocks too. But if you want to leverage on my time, knowledge, and expertise, so that you can have an easier route to your financial freedom goal, here are three things you can do.

1. Join My Exclusive Community

It is a closed Facebook group for individuals and couples who want to build strong finances and relationships at the same time.

I have also invited some of the best relationship coaches in Singapore to share insights to improve our relationships.

I'll personally share exclusive financial-related content meant for couples.

"Here's the link >> https://www.facebook.com/groups/lovemoneycommunity/"

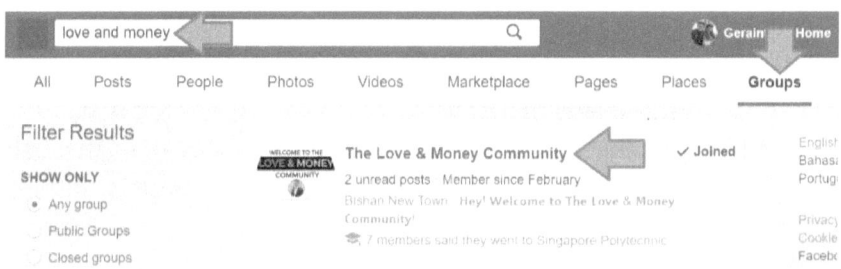

2. Watch My YouTube Videos

I post videos on the topics of finances and relationships every week on my YouTube channel, and there is one specific series I would like to introduce. It is called the "Investing for Beginners" series, where I talk about what you need to know before investing.

Here's the link >> http://bit.ly/InvestingForBeginnersPlaylist

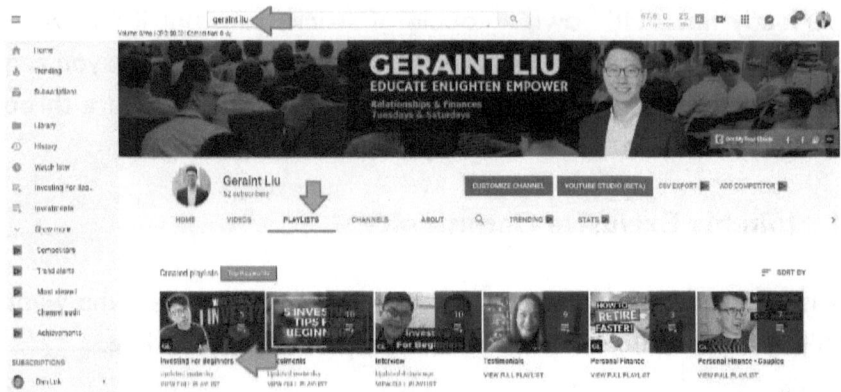

3. Take Action

Remember this quote from Tony Robbins at the start of the book? "Knowledge is **NOT** Power, it is only *POTENTIAL* Power, Action is Power".

We can acquire as much knowledge as we want, but nothing changes until we take action.

If you feel ready to take the next step and have someone to guide you along this journey, I have created "SPEED investing program" (SIP) to help you accelerate your path to your financial goals through safe investing strategies, without your spending any time or effort.

SPEED stands for:

Self Awareness

Position Your Goals

Evaluate Your Options

Establish A Plan

Dominate Your Goals

It represents a framework I've used to plan for hundreds of individuals, couples, and families to help them achieve their financial goals. It has given them clarity, certainty, and confidence as to what they want to achieve in life and how they plan to achieve it.

Check out some of the many testimonials the people I've worked with have given me.

https://www.geraintliu.com/reviews-and-testimonials/.

If you are keen to have someone guiding you through this investing journey, you can reach out to me through either of the following methods:

1. Drop me an e-mail at geraint.liu.lh@gmail.com
2. Private message me through any of my social media platforms.

Facebook Profile Page: https://www.facebook.com/geraintliulh

Facebook Business Page: https://www.facebook.com/GeraintLiu/

Instagram: https://www.instagram.com/geraintliu/

Linkedin: https://www.linkedin.com/in/geraintliu/

Remember, your life doesn't change if you don't take action on your new found knowledge.

Happy Investing!

About the Author

Geraint Liu is a financial strategist with one of the leading financial institutions in the world, specializing in helping couples invest safely so they can spend more quality time together.

He witnessed his loved ones suffer from poor financial advice and being burnt by trusting the wrong people. As a result, he dedicated his life to pursuing his vision and mission of creating a financially educated, empowered, and enlightened society, where everyone helps each other by paying forward what they have learnt.

He wrote this book to help as many people as possible invest safely and make more informed decisions.

Geraint is the creator of the "Financial Freedom Program" (FFP), a sixty-minute consultation to help families achieve financial freedom and the author of *Accelerate Your Path to Financial Freedom*.

www.ingramcontent.com/pod-product-compliance
Lightning Source LLC
Chambersburg PA
CBHW021043180526
45163CB00005B/2256